Acknowledgements

The original idea for this walk came from The Salter's Hill charity, which has three homes for adults with learning difficulties and for whom I have worked for many years.

Several towns in my home county of Gloucestershire have circular trails which also attract charity walks but not, until recently, Ross on Wye. A percentage of the cover price for each book sold will be passed on to Salter's Hill.

Salter's Hill

Meeting Individual Needs

**Salter's Hill Barn, Keepers Cottage,
Falcon Lane, Ledbury, HR 8 2JN**

I am indebted to members of both The Ross Ramblers and also members of Cheltenham Rambling club who have walked over many stages and helped with the new route planning. I am also very grateful to my wife Linetha, who continues to put up with my many absences from home, and who kindly agreed to proof read this new edition.

FRONT COVER: Wild horses on May Hill Common. " Hundred' trees on summit beyond.

ESCAPE
to the great outdoors!

A huge range of items for every sort of outdoor activity...

...from socks to Swiss Army knives and tents to torches

3 Croft Street
Ross on Wye

Tel: **01989 565676**

Striding Around Ross

by

Guy Vowles

CONTENTS	PAGE
Acknowledgements	3
Contents	5
Introduction	7-9
Ross - Past and Present	11
The Original Ross Round	12-30
including centrefold map of all walks	28-29
The Ultimate Ross Round	31-42
The New May Hill Loop	43-45
The Alternative Return from Ross to Weston	46-48
The Loughpool Loop	49-54
Services and Additional Information	55

Welcome to
ROSS-ON-WYE
a 'Walkers Are Welcome' town

An ideal base to explore the Wye Valley Walk, the Herefordshire Trail, the Ross Round and the rest of beautiful Herefordshire

The Ross-on-Wye Walkers are Welcome Group is a community based voluntary organisation that works to strengthen all aspects of walking for the benefit of visitors and residents alike, one of a network of over 100 towns and villages nationwide. Maps and guides have been published, an annual Walking Festival established and grants obtained to replace stiles with gates on local footpaths. A number of visiting groups of walkers have been helped with planning walks, accommodation and events.

If you would like assistance with a group visit or require any further information please contact us via our website or enquire at the Market House Visitor Centre.

PUBLICATIONS AVAILABLE AT:

Ross Old Books	**The Market House**	**Escape**	**Rossiter Books**
51 & 51 High Street	Visitor Centre	Croft Court	7 High Street

PROGRAMME OF WALKS FOR THE ROSS WALKING FESTIVAL • A GUIDE TO THE BUGGY ROUTE • A GUIDE TO DOG-FRIENDLY WALKS
ROSS-ON-WYE STREET MAP • ROSS AREA FOOTPATHS MAP • BUS WALKS IN AND AROUND ROSS

www.ross-on-wyewalkersarewelcome.co.uk

The Walks

The Original Ross Round (ORR) which was opened in 2004 was designed to utilise most of the best topographical and scenic features within a few miles around the town. It has certainly been well received by local walkers and others from far afield. Since the original production the author has been exploring additional possibilities and in this new book we are pleased to offer, not only the original walk, but a number of other longer and shorter options, that could provide nearly a week of good walking.

The author is now also an active member of the LDWA (Long Distance Walking Association) and with those members in mind we have added an extra loop over May Hill which, combined with much of the ORR now makes The Ultimate Ross Round (URR) a marathon distance- 42.5km (26m). This new loop can also be walked separately and, with two short connecting stretches from and back to Weston under Penyard, it makes a good 24km (15m) circular walk.

We have also formulated a new loop to the north of the river Wye which we are calling The Loughpool Loop. This uses the first 6km of the ORR before crossing the river at Foy and proceeding to the Loughpool Inn and returning to Ross via Peterstow and Wilton. This attractive walk is 19.2km (12m). Lastly we are describing our original shorter route from Weston under Penyard back to Ross in reverse so that walkers based in Ross can walk out on this and possibly return on the last stage of the ORR which makes a circular walk of 17km. (10.75m)

Since the last booklet, the main bus service between Ross and Gloucester is now running at mostly one hour intervals so that this service is very useful for leaving or joining the URR or the ORR at either Boxbush or Weston which provides more possibilities for shorter walks.

The routes are totally on official rights of way but do include a small proportion of road walking (mostly quiet lanes) The Loughpool Loop is the flattest walk but all the others have a few climbs. The route is certainly suitable for accompanied dogs, but given the agricultural countryside, they should certainly be on leads, particularly when in the proximity of farms with animals.

There are quite a few stiles, mostly in good condition, but regrettably few with separate canine apertures so that any dog needs to be as fit as it's owner!

Distances – Metric or imperial?

Although we are all used to miles, it is a fact that ordnance survey maps are metric based and, for those of us that did not know, every square is a kilometre. An old realistic pace for walking is about 2.5 miles per hour, which conveniently converts to 4km an hour or in fact one kilometre for every quarter of an hour. Hence walkers using the kilometre distances shown in the text should easily be able to calculate timings for arrival, etc.

A psychological point of view is that, rather like driving on the continent, the distances with kilometre walking tend to be realized rather more easily!

All of the walks are waymarked with the distinctive green and yellow ROSS ROUND discs and stickers but apart from the excellent maps in the book, walkers wishing to study 'the wider picture' should have either OS Landranger No 162, or the rather better OS Explorer OL14 which has more detail.

We hope that you will enjoy whichever part of these walks that you choose, whether it be the whole ultimate challenge or one of the shorter versions.

Public Rights of Way

All of the original route and now also The Loughpool Loop lie within the jurisdiction of The Herefordshire County Council, who have received a map and details of the walks as have Gloucestershire County Council who cover most of the new May Hill loop.

A number of difficult stiles and also problems with crops covering paths have been reported to both county councils. Walkers who experience further problems are urged to contact the respective footpath officer (preferably by email or post) quoting the exact location of any problem with an OS map reference and map type and number.

Herefordshire County Council,
Rights of Way Officer, c/o M/s Amery,
Unit 3, Thorn Business Park, Rotherwas Industrial Estate,
Hereford HR2 6JT
Email : streets@herefordshire.gov.uk

Gloucestershire County Council
Public Rights of Way Team, Shire Hall, Gloucester GL1 2TH
Email: prow@gloucestershire.gov.uk

THE WHITE HOUSE GUEST HOUSE

WYE STREET · ROSS-ON-WYE
HEREFORDSHIRE HR9 7BX

Tel/Fax: 01989 763572
Email: whitehouseross@aol.com
Website: www.whitehouseross.com

Ross Old Book & Print Shop

Books Bought and Sold
*Telephone: **01989 567458***

51 & 52 High Street, Ross-on-Wye, Herefordshire HR9 5HH
Email: chris@rossoldbooks.co.uk
A selection of books for sale at **www.rossoldbooks.co.uk**

Broome Farm
Peterstow
near Ross-on-Wye

home of the
Ross-on-Wye Cider & Perry Co

Open weekdays 2pm – 5pm
Weekends & Bank Holidays 10am – 5pm

Traditional Herefordshire Cider Fruit Farm

Our farmhouse cider and perry is made in the traditional way from 100% whole fruit juice from apples and pears grown on the farm.
Once pressed the juice is allowed to ferment in it's own natural yeasts.

– taste and buy our cider & perry straight from the barrels in the Cider Cellar
– take a stroll around the orchards and say hello to our lovely alpacas
– enjoy a Cream Tea (call 01989 562824 for availability)

Wooden Barrels for sale
01989 567232
www.rosscider.com

ROSS

Past and Present

The town was renamed 'On Wye' as recently as 1931, but could easily have been 'Ross on High' since the town sits so high above the river and, fittingly, the old English translation of 'Ross' actually means a promontory.

The siting of the town was probably governed by the crossing of the river at Wilton, which had existed since before Roman times. Indeed, at one time Wilton threatened to be larger than Ross but ultimately, due to flooding on the low lying and wet ground, a larger settlement grew up above the sandstone cliffs, which was by the time of Domesday a village with a manor granted to the Bishops of Hereford.

Ross soon emerged as a Market Town with a charter granted by King Stephen in the 12th century. The present, and recently refurbished, Market House was erected in the mid – 17th century and by this time local industries were flourishing with milling and tanning to the fore. In the early 19th century traffic on the River Wye had increased and this, combined with the advent of the railway, helped to foster increasing visitors to the town now known as "The Gateway to the Wye Valley".

Today visitors to the town can still appreciate many of the old buildings particularly several old Inns and, of course, the original St Mary's Church with it's neighbouring prospect gardens laid out by the town's great 17th Century benefactor, John Kyrle, immortalised as 'The Man of Ross'.

The town still enjoys a once weekly Market Day and has all modern facilities, shops, restaurants, a modern library, and an efficient Information Centre, fittingly situated in The Market House, to cope with all the daily influx of visitors requiring different facilities.

The Original Ross Round

STAGE 1
Ross Riverside – The Moody Cow at Upton Bishop

Distance
11.0 km (7 miles) – allow 2.25 – 3.0 hours

Terrain
Easy going – first 6 km on Wye Valley Walk with few stiles, later through pasture and a little woodland.

The walk commences on the river Wye close to the Riverside Inn. This is below the town centre and also accessible from Wilton Road. There is also a long term (free) car park further out on the Wilton Road, with a connecting low pedestrian tunnel under the road to facilitate access to the riverside walk area.

At the riverside concrete path and by the Wye Valley walk sign, turn right and follow the river upstream, soon passing another good pub The Hope and Anchor. Pass a modern and avant garde sculpture 'Flying Swans' designed by local craftsman Walenty Pytel.

Soon after, the path then takes a deviation around the Ross Rowing Club, which is to the left. This involves crossing a small footbridge into a playing field, at which turn left and follow the boundary around the Rowing Club to pick up the main river path. Head for the large concrete bypass bridge ahead **(1km)** where, after passing under, continue on the same rutted track for nearly a km, where there is a fork with a choice of way marking. Turn right to a double telegraph pole with electrical box in the centre and then turn left on to a wide track, previously the Hereford to Gloucester railway **(2km)**.

After about 500m the disused railway line is crossed by another track coming from the village of Brompton Abbot, but continue straight on for 200m, and look out for a way marked stile down into a field on the right. At which point leave the old railway line to cross the stile and

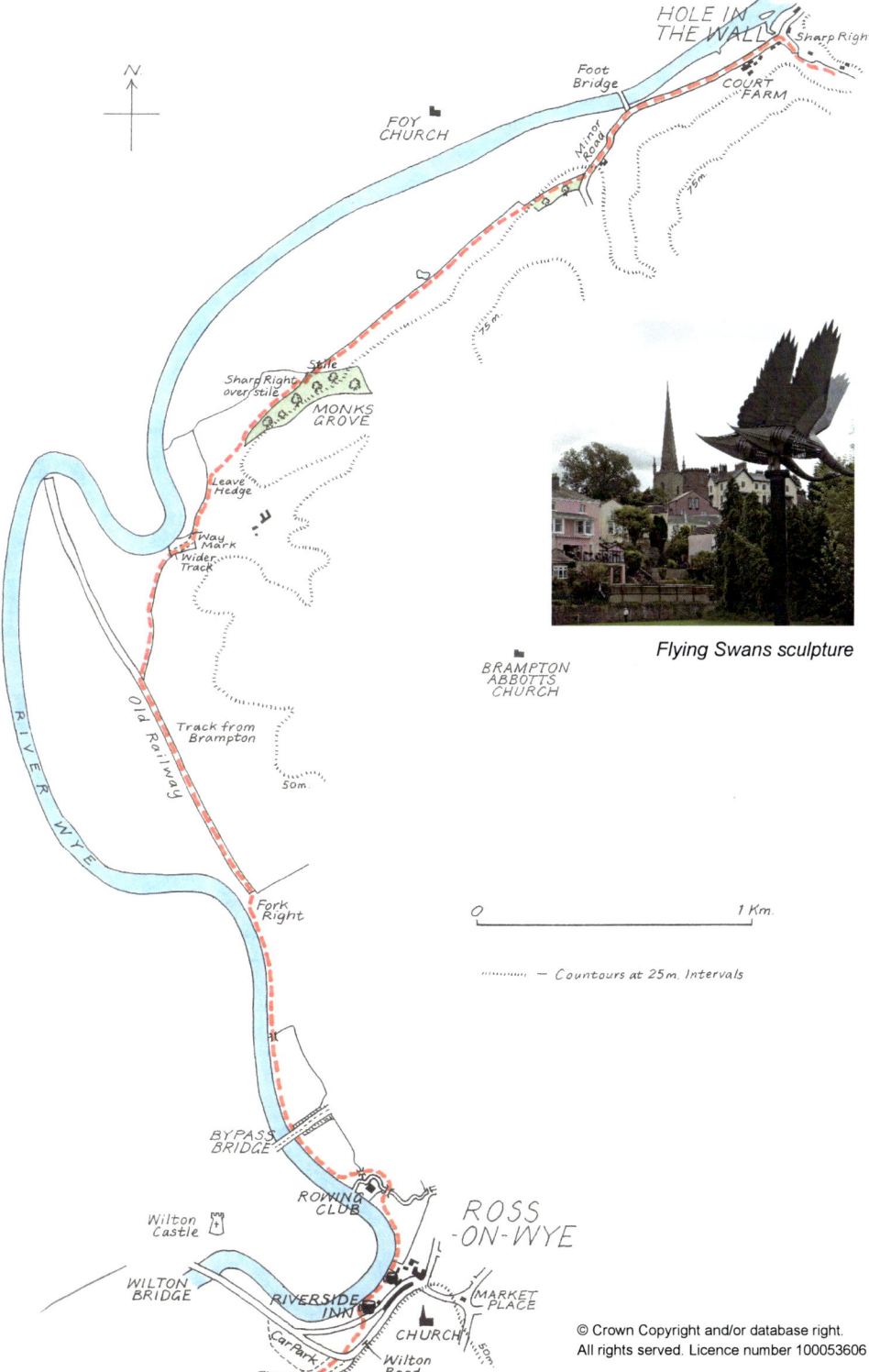

follow the boundary hedge on the right for about 500m **(3km)** until arriving at a wider track, once more adjacent to the river.

Continue on straight ahead for a further 80m to a way mark post at which turn left into a field but keep to the right of the hedge in front. After about 300m the field opens out, so leave the hedge and continue on the headland bearing right towards the woodland ahead. Continue on the left hand side of the woodland (Monks Grove) **(4km)** and after a further 200m arrive at the end of the field. Just before this, turn sharp right over another stile, with a way mark, into the wood and follow the path for nearly 100m to emerge at a metal kissing gate and into a large field. Continue forward, close to the left hand boundary and towards a pair of metal gates ahead into the next field. Visible over to the left, and in fact over the river, is the interesting little church at the hamlet of Foy. (see Loughpool Loop Walk)

Bypass the first set of gates and cross a stile to the right of the second pair of gates and proceed on over more pasture **(5km)** following close to the fence line on the left until nearly at the end of the field. Bear right uphill to arrive at the edge of woodland where, under a large oak tree, find a metal gate with separate pedestrian gate.

Pass through and into the wood where the enclosed path (can be overgrown at times) emerges after 500m at a minor road. Turn left down the road and after a further 200m, pass (but do not cross, unless walking The Loughpool Loop) the interesting large and sprung footbridge over the river. Continue on the road for a further 500m to a collection of farm buildings, Court Farm, on the right - now owned by PGL (Leisure) Holidays. This is Hole in the Wall. **(6km)**

Just past the buildings leave The Wye Valley Walk and at the little 'green' with a post box, turn right - FP sign marked Upton Bishop and Brampton Abbots- and proceed through a narrow little path to a stile and cross into lush pasture. Keep close to the left boundary and continue up towards post and rail fencing in the distance, with a nice half timbered house on the left. Beyond this house, but out of sight, is the original home of the Clive family (of India fame).

Continue through two gates **(7km)** and on up this attractive and quiet valley still keeping close to the left boundary fence. Reach another gate with a stile alongside and continue ahead with the woodland now close on both sides until you reach a positive track way where turn right and start climbing (first but not last climb of the day!) up into the woodland.

Reach a clearing at the top, passing a private track to the right, and proceed on for a few metres to reach a T junction where turn right down an enclosed track way between hedges **(8km)**. This is almost a vehicular track which continue on about 400m to reach The Burnt House (Civil War connections) and then the main A449 Ross – Ledbury road.

Cross very carefully over this busy road to double metal gates and proceed ahead on the double track with fine views ahead and follow the left hand boundary through two fields before turning sharp right, still admiring the views. where one can see the spire of Ross Parish church away on the right and the wooded slopes of Howle Hill to the left of the town **(9km)**. Continue with a hedge on the left, through a further field, where the track becomes enclosed (rather like an old drove road) and continue down to Wobage Farm. (Craft workshops)

Just before the buildings there is a track way to the left but ignore this and bear right down to the right hand corner of the buildings , where there is access onto a well manicured gravel driveway with two way marking signs clearly in front. Follow the driveway around and out to the other side of the buildings and down the tarmac drive **(10km)** to the B4224 road. Cross very carefully and climb the narrow stile opposite into the field beyond.

Turn right and follow the hedge down to a stile at the bottom of the field which cross and then turn left and pass through a gate into the next field. The route bears slightly right and down over rough and boggy ground to a planked bridge and then up to the top right hand corner of the field. Arrive at a stile and cross into the next field to continue ahead following the right hand boundary. After 200m the gradient levels out and a gate is reached with a choice of routes **(10.5km)**. The direct route is straight ahead but those wishing to visit the elegant Moody Cow pub in the village – called Upton Bishop, but marked on the map as Crow Hill, should cross the stile on the right and continue straight over two small fields until a stile is found in the right hand side of the second field and this gives access to a narrow path which leads out on to a minor road. Here turn right up to the crossroads and the pub is immediately ahead. The deviation is approx 500m of additional walking each way.

The Local No 32 bus service between Upton Bishop and Ross runs about every 2 hours and the bus stop is about 100m further up the road from the pub. The pub can also arrange for taxis to collect tired walkers!

Bollitree Castle

The Original Ross Round

STAGE 2
The Moody Cow pub to The Weston Cross Inn at Weston under Penyard

Distance
6.5km (4.06m) – allow 1.5 – 2.0 hours without stops

This is a short varied section with initial agricultural land but once under the M50 motorway, there is an interesting lakeside passage and then quiet lane walking followed by more fields. Bollitree Castle provides a scenic focal point before the descent down to The Weston Cross Inn.

From the front of The Moody Cow pub, cross carefully over the staggered crossroads and head towards the red phone box. Just before this turn left up an enclosed track to a stile, which cross and continue alongside the left hand boundary hedge to a further stile. Continue on the same line over two more stiles to reach the main route. Turn right and follow the hedge and after 300m arrive at a post and rail fence with a stile on the right.

Cross into a further field and after 50m arrive at another stile. Cross this and continue on an enclosed track behind buildings for approx 50m before turning left up to a minor road. Turn right down to a staggered crossroads and continue straight across (SP Linton – Newent), taking care, since the crossing below on the right is blind.

After 25m turn right at a sign marked Oatlands, pass post and rail fencing, **(11km)** and carry straight on down between hedges to a minor road (B4221), where cross over onto the access drive to Felhampton Farm. This leads directly to the very old and attractive half timbered farmhouse where continue on between the buildings to a second gate and then through into a field with a boundary fence on the right. Pass a small pond on the right and continue through a further gate towards a bungalow ahead. Just before this cross a stile

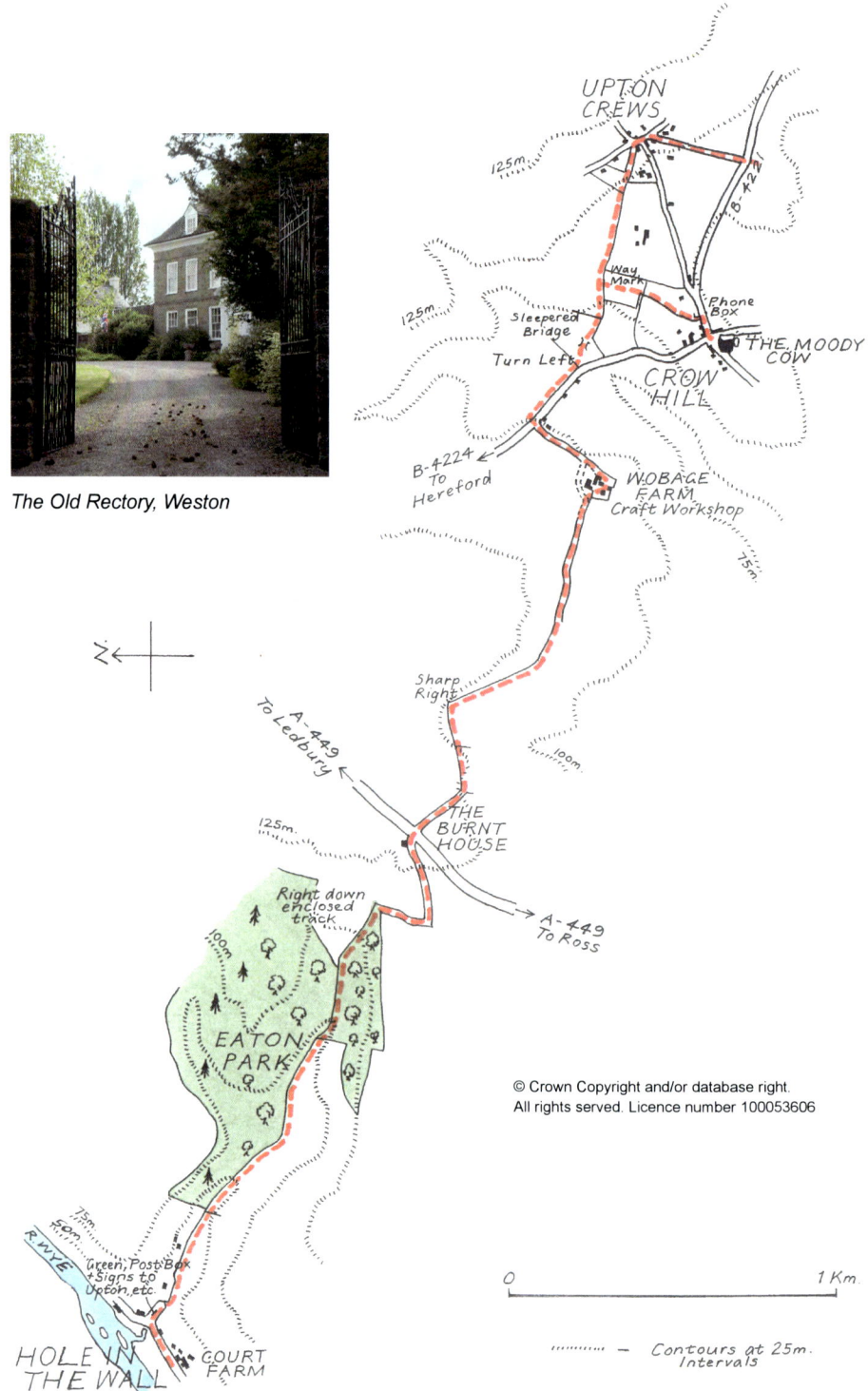

on the left and continue ahead with a hedge on the left to cross firstly, a single stile, and then a double stile to arrive on the edge of a very large field with good views ahead over Hartleton Water and with May Hill in the distance **(12km)**.

Cross the stile and make for the distant corner of the field opposite with way mark hopefully visible. Cross the stile with a boundary hedge and the busy M50 now on the right hand side. Continue initially down hill but then rise up the other side to a stile in the right hand corner. Just the other side of the stile turn right on a gravelled track which passes under the motorway and continue downhill between the lakes with the buildings on the right being another P.G.L. holiday centre site **(13km)**.

Pass a weir between the lakes and rise up to another trackway at which turn left. The whole area has been tastefully landscaped and includes new tree planting and flowers in the spring. Continue on and join a road by another metal sculpture similar to the one on the riverside at Ross. The road winds along parallel to the lake and arrives at a lodge with other attractive buildings nearby and a minor road beyond **(14km)**.

This is the point at which walkers doing The Ultimate Ross Round (URR) can turn left to go up to Linton and on up and over May Hill but otherwise walkers following The Original Ross Round (ORR) turn right up this narrow road. This ascends steadily for nearly a kilometre to reach a T junction at the top but do keep a lookout for suitable 'stand aside' places, since any occasional vehicles can take up much of the road **(15km)**.

Cross the road at the top, turn right, and after 20m turn left through a gate with a way marking post alongside and then pass through a short enclosed area to a rusty gate with stile alongside. Continue over the next short field to cross a stile over post and rail fencing and continue on down by the left hand side of the next much larger field with views of the Welsh Black mountains in the distance. This area has many rabbit and fox burrows so beware where you tread.

The path arrives at the bottom left hand corner where cross a stile. Pass through a short grassy section with more burrows underfoot and arrive after 50m at a stile on the left. Bear right in the next very large field and make your way up to the left of a red bricked house on the ridge. This large field can often be in crop and it is adviceable to find a 'line' between plantings that proceeds in the general direction.

Arrive at a double metal gate to the left of the house **(16km)** and emerge onto a minor road. Turn right and walk up to the hamlet of Bollitree with it's mock castle façade and moat at the front. There are several legends as to the origin of the castle but the most interesting one is that a farmer who owned the farmhouse was attempting to woo a Spanish lady of noble birth, who said that she would only consider him if he owned a castle. He duly made the improvements with the battlements you see today but regrettably the 'dear lady' still declined his offer of marriage.

Turn left into a narrow lane with 'the castle' now on the right. In fact peeping through the gates the farmhouse is visible beyond, and in itself is not insubstantial. Continue along this quiet lane passing the most impressive Old Rectory, with coat of arms on the front elevation, and continue on to another fine house on the right which is Bollitree Lawns. Just past this turn right onto a narrow Green Lane, now used as access for horses judging from the hoof marks although it can get quite overgrown at times.

The trackway narrows and bends around a corner to join an access lane to Rose Cottage on the left where turn right and walk downhill to a minor road. Turn left and continue on to the welcoming Weston Cross Inn **(17km)**.

Walkers wishing to finish the walk here can use the Ross to Gloucester bus service (mostly every hour) which stops on either side of the A40 by the pub.

The Original Ross Round

STAGE 3
Weston Inn – Riverside at Ross 12km (7.5miles)
allow 3.0 - 3.5 hours walking time.

This is probably the most interesting stage of the ORR but definitely the most strenuous. A gentle start through open fields, then a climb up through deciduous woods is followed by a short descent with another climb up to Howle Hill. There is then a final descent and easy walking back to Ross.

Leave the Weston Inn, cross the A40 road carefully, and proceed up the lane diagonally opposite. After about 200m the church will be reached on the left, where climb up the slope and steps, pass through the churchyard to the left of the church, and exit by a kissing gate. Turn right to another gate, and then bear left in the next small field to reach a stile.

Continue in the next field with houses on the left, to arrive at a metal gate with a small pedestrian gate alongside. Pass through this, cross a trackway and enter a field on the opposite side. The right of way is diagonally right (crops may obscure path) to a stile in the far hedgerow. The line is towards a stone barn on the hillside beyond. Reach the stile which cross carefully and also a hidden ditch. Turn left and walk along the headland following the hedge to find a stile in the corner of the field under trees **(18km)**. Cross this and continue following the hedge on the left as it curves around this long field to reach a double gate and a stile at the far end.

Arrive on the access trackway to the house opposite where turn left and follow it down to a minor road. This is the point where the URR from May Hill joins from the opposite lane. Turn right and continue straight ahead past a T junction (SP Kerne Bridge) until adjacent to Parkfields Country House, turn left off the road to find a stile. Bear right in the next field where the line is to the right of a black metalled barn but depending on the crops, either take a direct line across the field, or walk around the field by the right hand boundary.

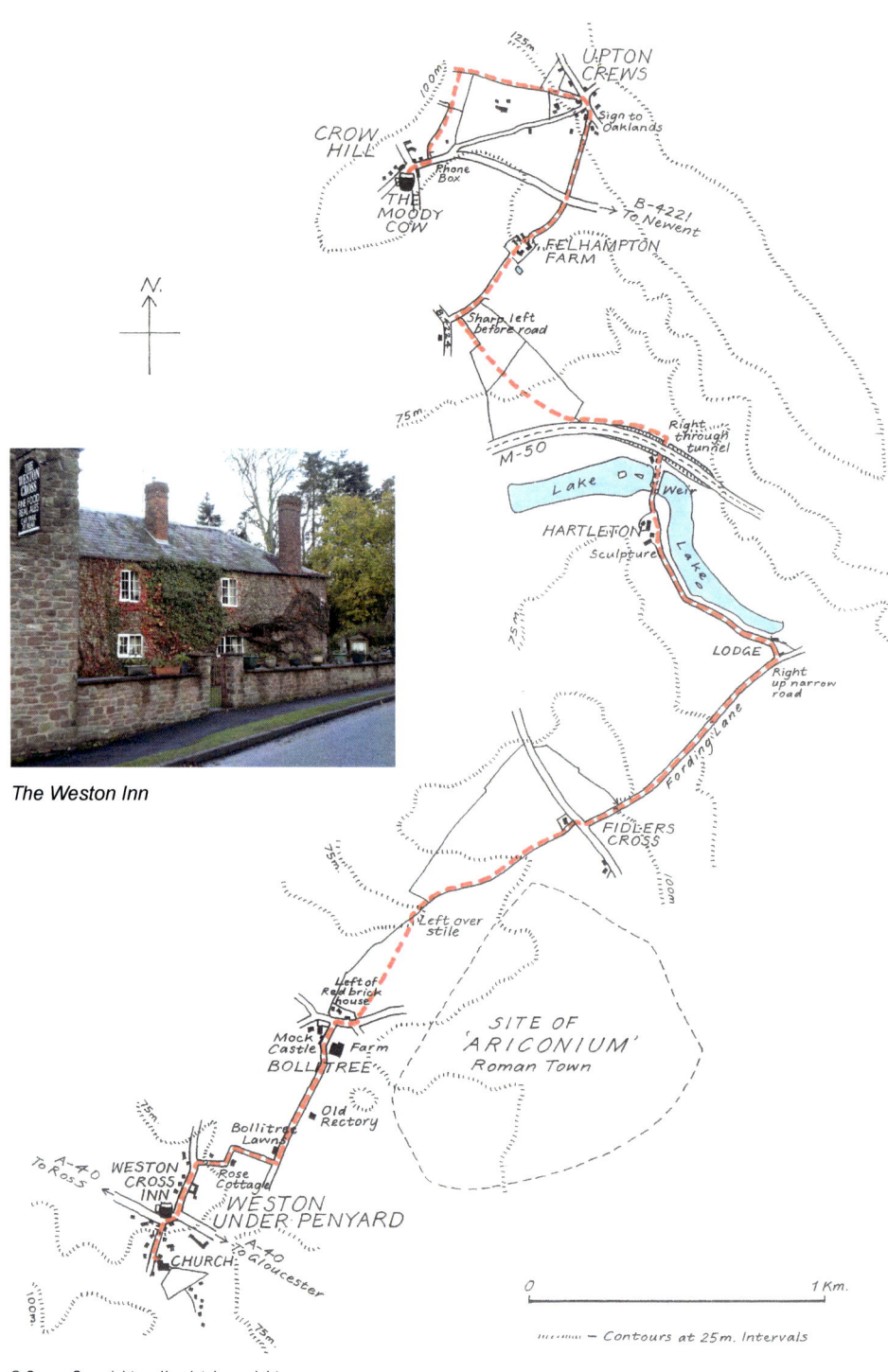

The Weston Inn

Beyond the barn and in front of a brick built bungalow is an access trackway where turn left and proceed up this enclosed way, which winds up quite steeply past several houses, until at the end a post barrier is reached. Continue past this and continue to climb steeply up through this attractive wood, which is covered in bluebells in the spring. The trackway levels out at the top, with a house on the right, and shortly after, turn right up a few steps set in a low wall and walk up to a stile set in a beech hedge **(19km)**.

Over the stile there are superb views down into the wooded valley and over further woodland to the surrounding hills. It's a good excuse for a little breather! before descending slightly left of centre, beyond a telegraph pole, down into the left hand corner of the field to a stile under trees. Cross the trackway below and descend immediately opposite, under more trees, into a hidden and attractive gully. This leads down after 100m to a narrow path which cross to a stile and emerge out into pasture beyond. Bear left down the field passing the attractive Lodge Farm on the right and continue past post and rail fencing to arrive at the bottom (right hand) end of the field with a gate and stile giving access to a lane beyond. Turn left on the lane and walk up to another lane where turn left **(20km)** to find a trackway on the right with way marking post.

Continue up this attractive sunken way to arrive at a clearing in the beech woods **(21km)** and continue up to the left of another way marking post to reach another sunken track. The gradient eventually levels out and is lovely woodland walking with views through the trees on the right. After 800m arrive at a short rocky incline and ascend up to a lane and a road junction.

Continue straight over and past a smart chalet bungalow, with a hedge and an archway at the front, before arriving alongside the old redundant Parish church, with adjacent schoolhouse. This is now the extensive area of Howle Hill where continue on, past the former 'Crown Inn' down on the right, to a fork in the lane. **(22km)** Bear right at a blue traffic sign and continue on around the bends to arrive at another chapel with a nice grassy area in front. (ideal for another rest?)

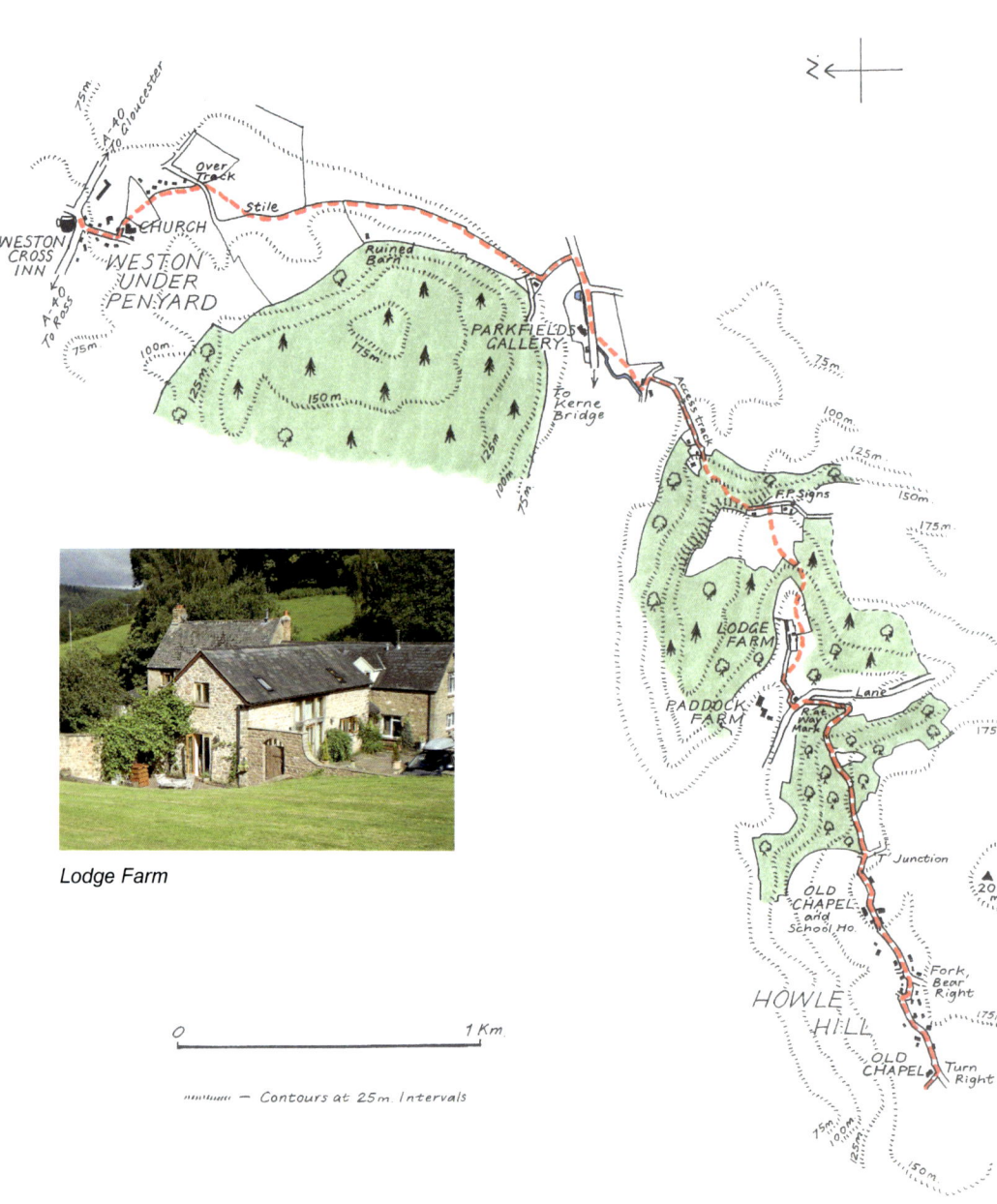

Lodge Farm

Turn right past the old chapel and walk up the lane to a white house with woodland beyond and a choice of footpaths. Take the left hand bridle path which soon starts descending and eventually arrives alongside a white cottage with a conservatory at the front. Continue down on the concrete trackway to arrive at a sign (Wye Valley Way) where bear left onto a stony track which passes in front of a large detached house with a brick wall at the front **(23km)**.

After 100m, take a sharp right turn down steps into woodland and continue over rough ground as the path winds down to arrive at a lane. Turn right and then almost immediately left to cross a stile. Follow the path on the left boundary to the corner where, at a chestnut tree, turn left and follow the boundary, past a little spring, down to an access road and a larger road beyond.

Turn right at the bend and walk down to the busy Walford – Ross road. Turn right and follow the pavement for 100m before crossing over carefully and taking a trackway SP – New House Farm that passes alongside a high wall and fencing in front of housing.

At the end of the houses continue straight ahead on a grassy footpath, which is rather attractive as it passes through a tunnel of bushes **(24km)**. At the end of the footpath cross a stile on the left into a large field and immediately turn right and follow the hedgerow on the right to reach an open area. Bear left on the wide trackway, pass under power lines and continue ahead (500m) with arable fields on both sides to reach a lane **(25km)**.

Turn right, and after 100m turn left by an old black painted gate to pass down a stony trackway which joins the driveway to Old Hill Court, a very attractive (medieval origins) house. Continue up the tarmac drive, exit through a gateway onto a minor road, and turn right. Soon pass the impressive driveway to Hill Court, which is now the European headquarters of The Rehau Group. Continue along the road, with a good traffic free verge in places, to pass a converted chapel on the right and then arrive at a junction where turn up left to a large farm complex, The Homme **(26km)**.

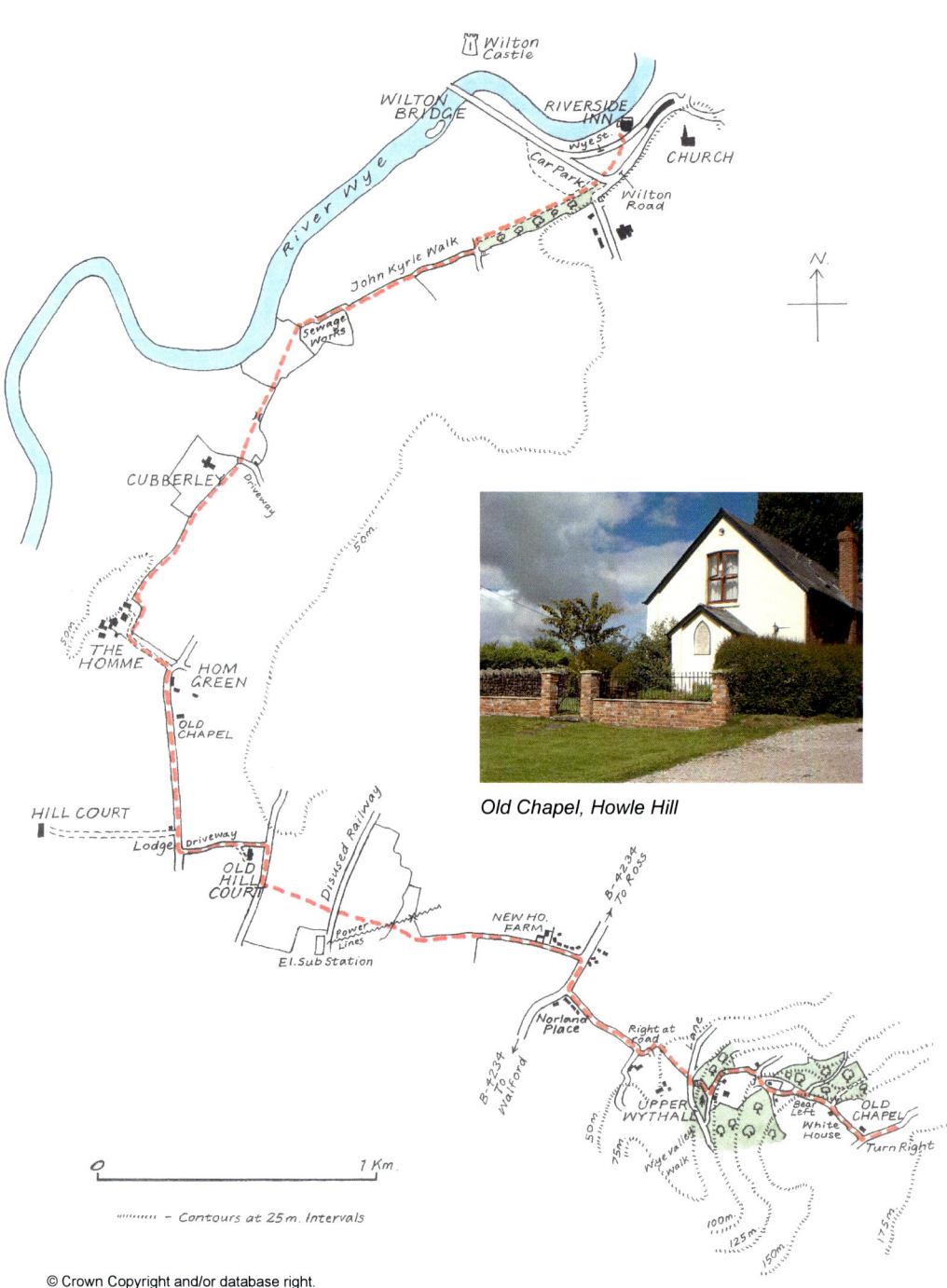

Old Chapel, Howle Hill

Fork right before the main buildings and then as a 'village' of caravans comes into view, climb up an embankment on the right, and continue ahead, through saplings, with the caravans now down on the left. At the end of the bank turn left for 25m, and then turn right to the hedge opposite. Continue on with the hedge on your left, past a prominent oak tree, and after 500m arrive at a stile in the corner of the field.

Arrive at the well kept boundary of Cubberley, a large renovated property once owned by Roger Whittaker. (the well known 'ballad' singer) Pass through an ornamental iron gate with a mown grassy walkway and emerge onto the driveway to the house **(27km)**.Cross over onto a similar well maintained pathway between post and rail fencing.

Continue to a large wooden footbridge and cross a stile beyond into a large field (may have crops obscuring footpath) where continue across, slightly left of centre, making for a copse of conifers on the opposite side. Arrive at a trackway where bear right past a way mark post, cross another track, and ascend up onto an enclosed track (John Kyrle Walk) to pass alongside a sewage works.

This becomes a narrower path, which rises up onto a headland with Ross church more prominent ahead. Continue with a hedge on the left as the path is later enclosed, until it eventually drops down steps to a wide path with steps on the opposite side **(28km)**

Turn left, but after a few metres bear right and continue on down to the edge of playing fields. Turn right alongside the playing fields and proceed towards the car park ahead, pass a skate boarding area with a road up ahead, but bear right to pass under the road. (low tunnel- can get flooded in winter- in which case take narrow footpath on right which emerges up onto main road to town centre) The official route arrives out of the tunnel onto a large grassy area with the fine bandstand in front and The Riverside Inn beyond **(28.8km)**

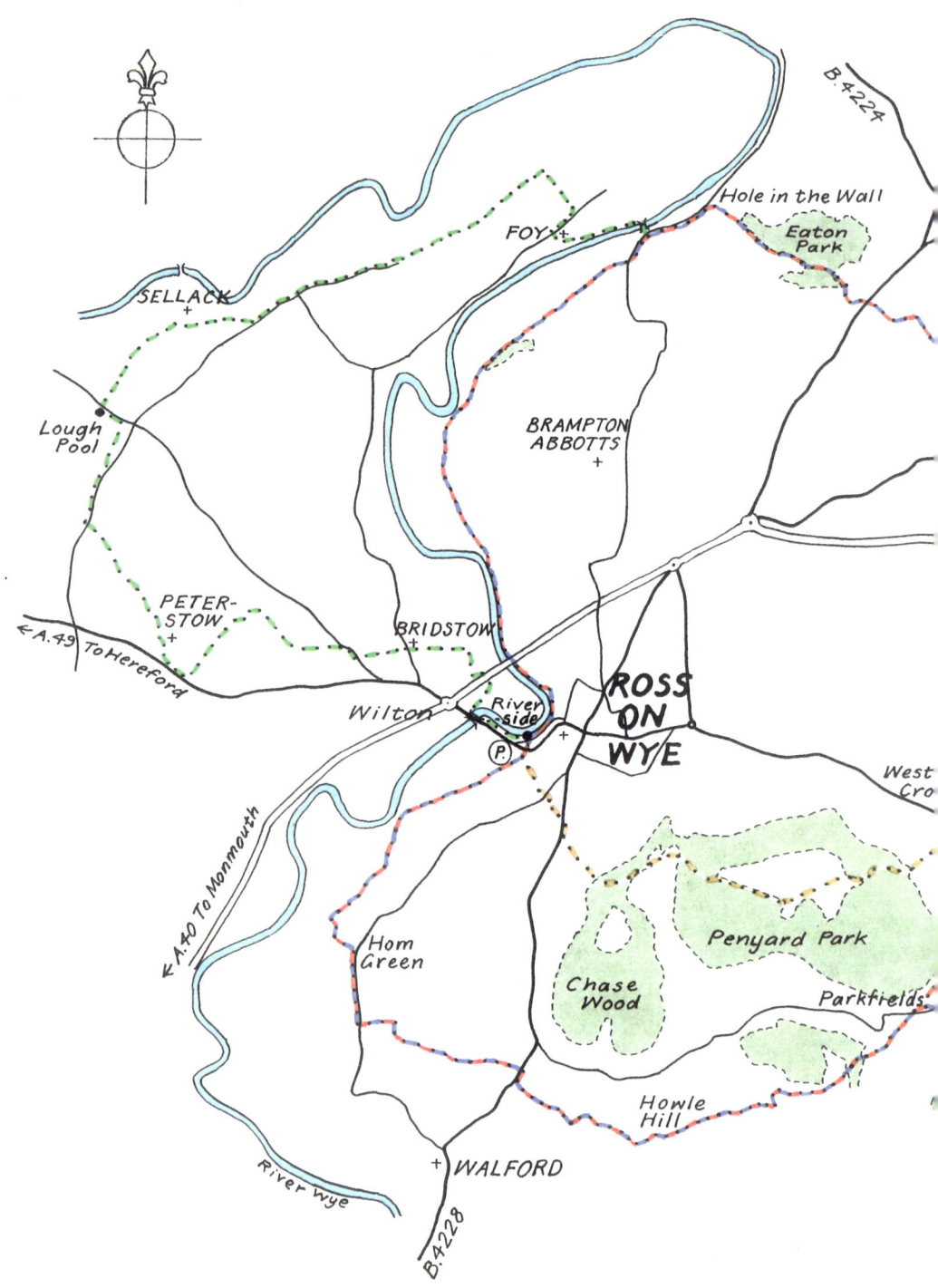

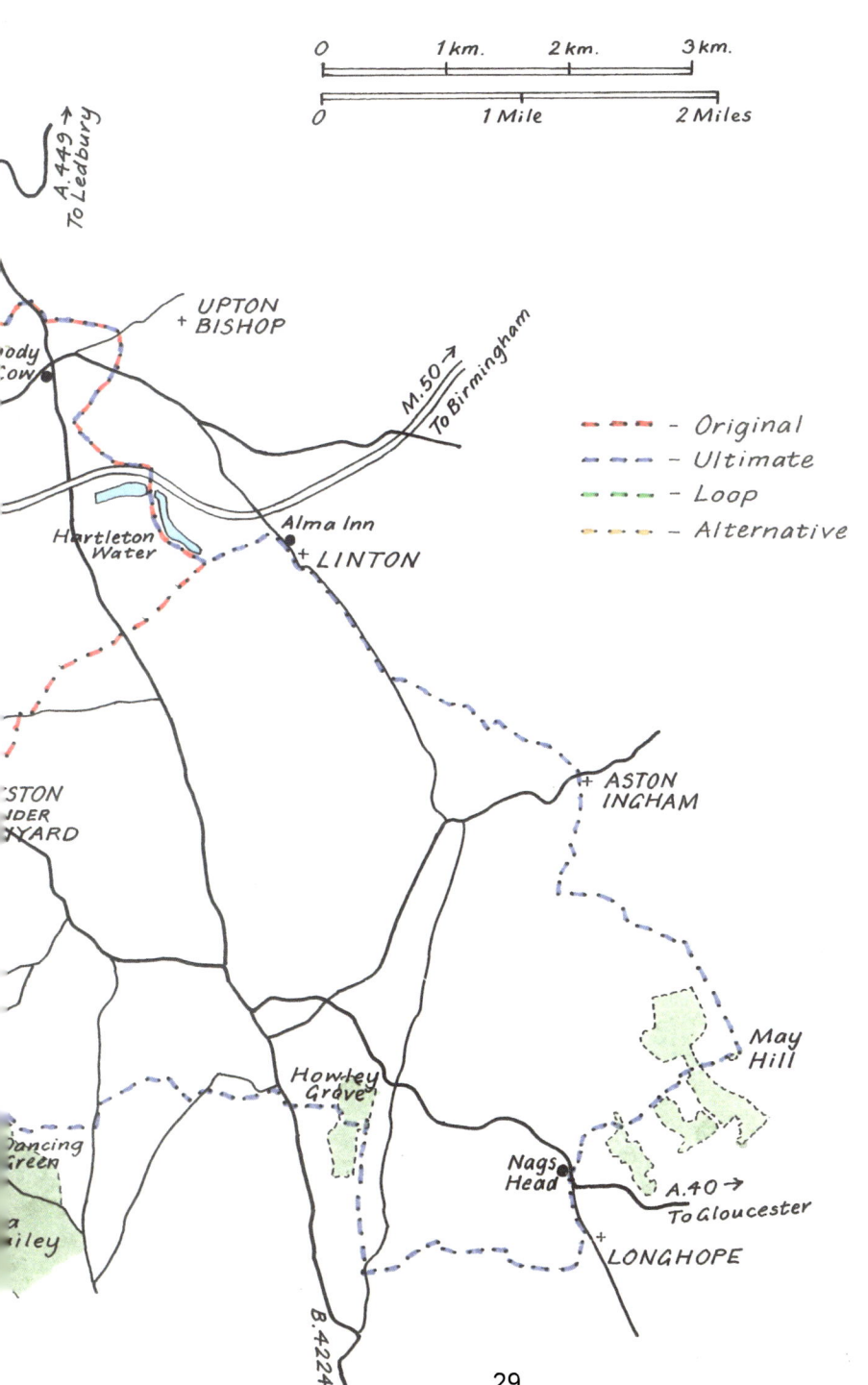

Foy Church

The Ultimate Ross Round (URR)

STAGE 1
ORR Riverside Ross – Hartleton Water Junct 13.5km (8.44m)
Allow 3.0- 3.5 hours without stops

STAGE 2
URR Hartleton – Box Bush (Nags Head Inn) 10.0 km (6.25m)
Allow 2.5-3.0 hours without stops

STAGE 3
URR Box Bush – Parkfields Country House 9.2 km (5.75m)
Allow 2.0-2.5 hours without stops

STAGE 4
ORR Parkfields – Ross Riverside 9.8 km (6.13m)
Allow 2.25- 3.0 hours without stops

TOTAL 42.5km (26.5m)
Allow 10.0-12.0 hours without stops.

This is an extension of the original Ross Round (ORR), with an extra loop around May Hill, that takes the overall distance up to a Marathon equivalent. However for those not wishing to walk this extreme distance in one day it is easily possible to do separate parts since there is the excellent Gloucester to Ross bus service which stops at both Box Bush and also Weston under Penyard (see May Hill Loop walk).

The new loop has much character with quite a lot of hill walking besides May Hill. There are a number of typical Herefordshire black and white cottages to admire and some nice deciduous woodland. There are regrettably a few large fields which, when planted with crops, can be difficult to traverse and we have mentioned deviations that can be followed.

*The distances for the new loop are shown separately to the distances on the first and last sections of The Original Ross Round and overall calculations for the whole Ultimate Ross Round are a cumulative total.

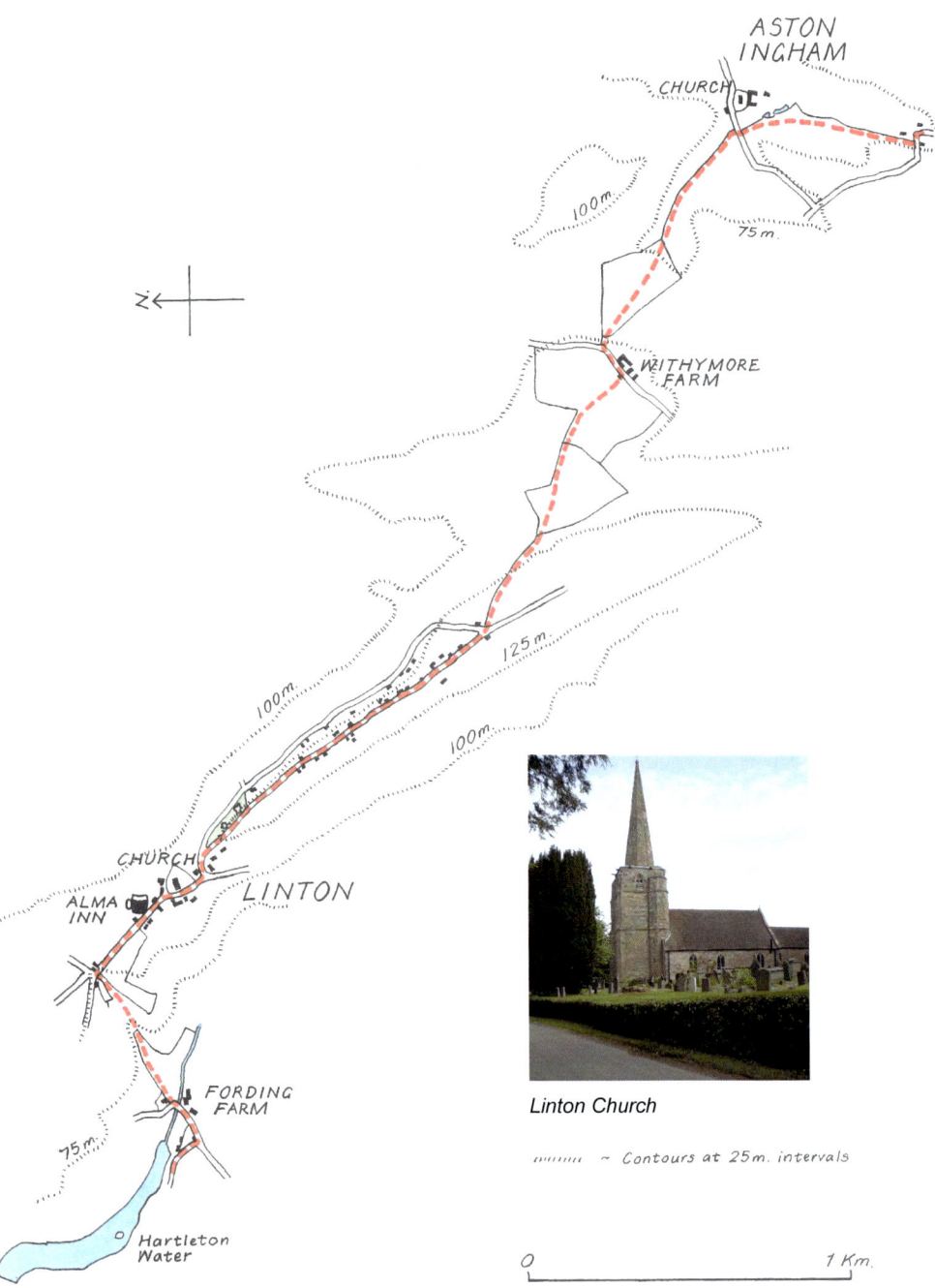

Linton Church

.... ~ Contours at 25m. intervals

STAGE 2
10.0 km (6.25m) allow 2.5 – 3.0 hours without stops.

At the junction with the lane from Hartleton Water TURN LEFT for the URR and walk downhill past Fording Farm to a left hand bend where cross a stile on the right. Continue ahead, close to the garden of the house on the left, and ascend the bank in front with a wooded gully now on the left. The bank levels out but continue up the field as it narrows and at the end cross to stone steps up to a stile on the right.
Turn left in the next field (easier up above the bank) and follow the left hand boundary up to the top of the field and find another stile. Cross this and follow the narrow path over a stream up to a minor road with a converted barn opposite. This is the village of Linton where turn right and follow the lane up to The Alma Inn. This unpretentious pub is famous for it's great selection of real ales but only occasionally offers food. It has an enormous garden where a very popular music festival is held once a year.

Continue up the lane, past the post office, and up to the church, with it's fine steeple **(1km)**. Climb the steps into the churchyard and pass through to the other side to emerge on a road with the village hall on the right. Turn left and walk up the road, ignoring a fork to the left, and gradually ascend the ridge with fine views opening up on either side **(2km)**. The road eventually arrives at a junction, with a grassy triangular green, where cross a stile opposite with a gate alongside and a good view of May Hill in the distance.
Continue ahead in the field with a boundary hedge on the left and arrive at another stile in the bottom left hand corner (obscured) Cross the stile and in the next field walk ahead across the field to reach the opposite hedgerow by a prominent oak tree. Follow the hedge on your left to a gateway with rusty old metal gate **(3 km)** Pass through and after about 70m bear right past a large dead elm tree towards the farm ahead. Pass through a metal gate and onto a lane with Withymore Farm opposite (B&B facilities).

Turn left on the lane and after 100m turn right and pass through two gates into a large field. The right of way is diagonally right down to

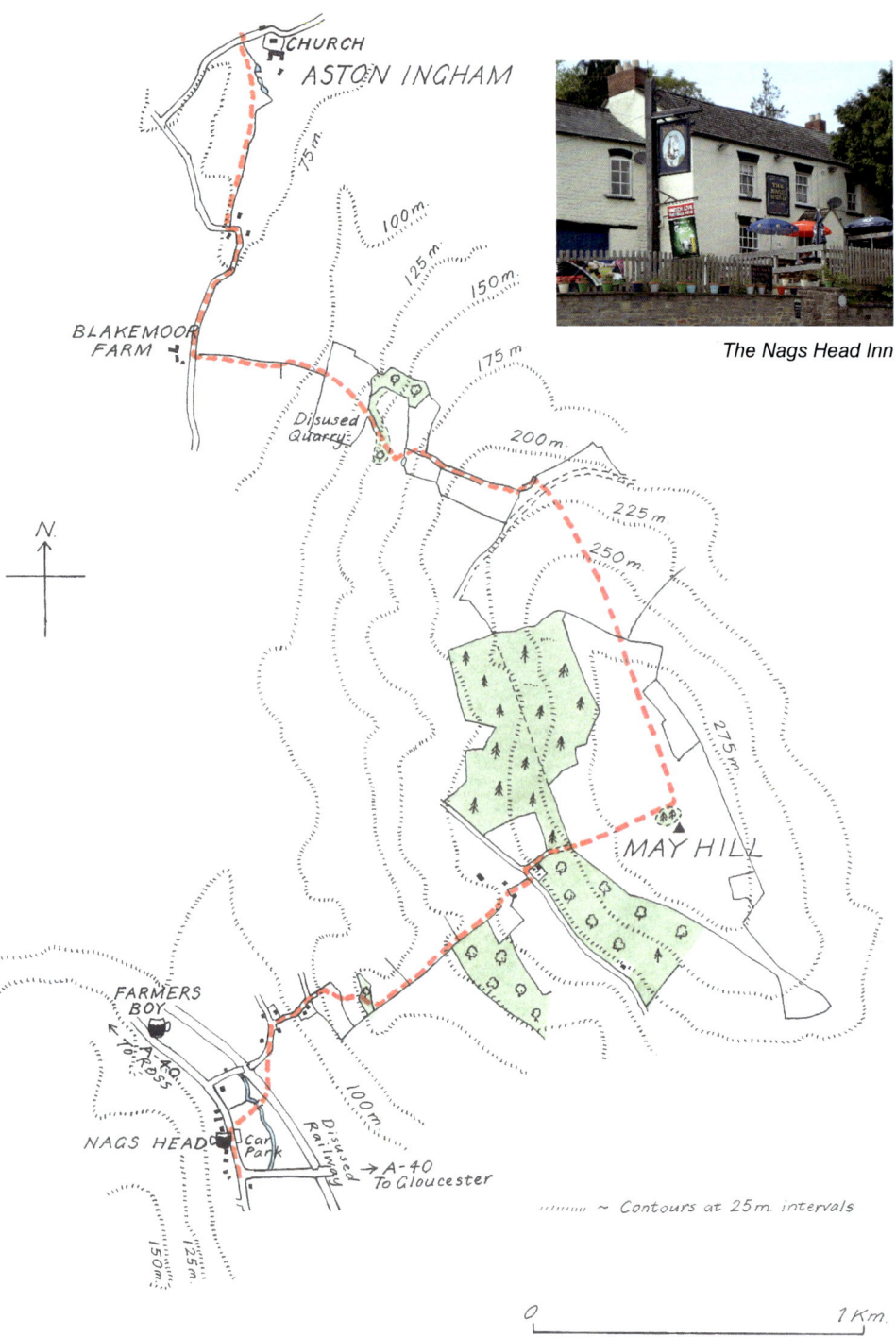

The Nags Head Inn

the far corner but if the field is in crop it may be preferable to follow the left hand boundary around the field. Arrive at a muddy gap in the corner and cross the stream into the next field where follow the left hand boundary over two stiles, with metal gates, to a lane **(4km)**. This is the village of Aston Ingham, and if with time permitting, you fancy a break, it is worth while taking a small deviation to the attractive church on the left which has a nice bench outside. You will also notice a well with nicely built stone cover just below the bench. The route continues on the opposite side of the gate and stile and the path follows the left hand boundary of this enormous field and winds around to eventually reach another lane **(5km)**.

Turn left on the lane and then bear right as you pass a black and white house called The Dane. Continue on the lane for 500m until opposite Blakemoor Farm, turn off left, initially on a trackway towards a large pylon, but before this, bear left and walk up to the top left hand corner of the field to find an obscured stile.

Cross the stile and turn right up along a narrow enclosed footpath to reach another stile. Continue steeply up the next field to reach another obvious stile on the edge of woodland. Cross this and arrive on a good vehicular trackway. **(6km)** Turn right and walk up and past a small quarry where, soon after, bear left up to a new metal gate with stile alongside. Turn right in the next field and ascend up to a gap on the right (old gate alongside) and continue on the same line up into the middle of the next field.

As the gradient levels out, bear left across the field to reach the boundary hedge of the adjoining field and follow this up to a stile in the top left hand corner. (do not be tempted to walk up towards parked cars up on the right of the field- no access) Cross the stile and walk through the plantation to reach a minor road and a tall way marking post. Cross over to a narrow footpath that winds up through silver birch trees to reach a wider path. Turn left and follow this uphill past more scattered trees and eventually arrive at a prominent large gate and separate pedestrian gate alongside with May Hill prominent on the hillside above **(7km)**.

Continue on up to arrive at the famous clump of trees (a hundred Scots Pines originally planted to commemorate Queen Victoria's Jubilee) and pass them on the left to reach a trig point and amazing views into the distance and over the Severn estuary. Continue around the trees, pass a green painted bench, and arrive on the western side at a prominent way marking sign with more great views, this time, over to the Welsh mountains.

Turn left and make your way down through gorse bushes towards a large larch plantation. Arrive at a wooden gate and continue down, later on steps, to emerge on a lane **(8km)** with a rather nice timber framed house on the left. Turn left on the lane, and then after 30m turn right, to cross over a stile (sp Gloucestershire Way). Continue on down, following the boundary on your right, to reach another stile which cross and turn left to follow the left hand boundary. Ignore a gateway on your left but continue ahead to drop down with the boundary still on the left to reach another stile. Continue on the same line to reach a further stile with woodland beyond.

Enter the woodland, cross a further stile **(9km)** and emerge on the far side into a narrow field. Cross this to reach another stile and drop down steps to a field. Turn right, walk alongside new fencing to a way marking post and then follow the enclosed footpath as it drops down quite steeply, past a metal gate, to a lane.

Turn left and follow it down past attractive cottages until it reaches a larger lane. Turn left and continue past The Old Farm (self catering cottages) and just by a road sign (low bridge ahead) take a footpath on the left. This passes through three metal gates as you cross over an old railway (Ross to Gloucester), drop down to reach a bridge over a stream and cross a meadow beyond, to reach the car park for The Nags Head Inn, which is beyond the very busy A40 road **(10km)**.
Note – The Nags Head has a reasonable range of beers and ciders and serves very good value food but opening hours can be limited. There is also the Farmers Boy pub which is 500m in the Ross direction and which offers a rather more extensive range of food. There is additionally a B&B in the pink house almost opposite this pub.

STAGE 3
Boxbush – Nags Head Inn to Parkfields Country House
9.2km (5.75m) allow 2.00- 2.5 hours without stops

With your back to the pub, turn RIGHT (Gloucester direction) and walk down the pavement to a road junction where leave the main road and turn off right onto the minor road (Longhope). After 500m cross a stile on the right into an arable field. The route is diagonally across to the top left corner but it may be necessary, with any full grown crop, to walk around the left hand boundary. Arrive at a stile with steep steps on the far side and descend to a trackway.

Turn right and walk up the trackway **(11km)** which winds around and then ascends up to Preece Moor Farm. Continue past the farmhouse and between outbuildings to a gate with grassy track beyond. This drops downhill between hedges and then ascends to another gate. Continue to climb in the field beyond, up a gulley between thorn bushes, to arrive at a gate at the top with fine views back over to May Hill on the far right. **(12 km)** Continue up another gully from the gate which soon levels out and the path then drops down past farm buildings, through a gate, and down to a lane. Cross the lane and pass through a gate into the field beyond with views of Mitcheldean town over to the left. Cross the field diagonally to a gap and then turn right and walk down alongside the hedge to a house with a gate into a driveway and lane beyond. **(13 km)**

Turn right and walk up to a corner. The route is over a stile and straight across the field opposite but this can often be in crop. (impassable maize) The farmer sometimes shows an alternative route around the inside of the field but this can also be difficult so, that in the worst scenario, it is often best to walk along the lane (right) to Bradley Farm and then to turn left and walk up to Laine's Farm to rejoin the official route. This would add on about 500m but would definitely be faster!

In the best conditions, cross the stile, and continue across the field past a ruined brick building to find an obscure stile in the far hedge (near pair of trees). Continue straight across the next grassy field

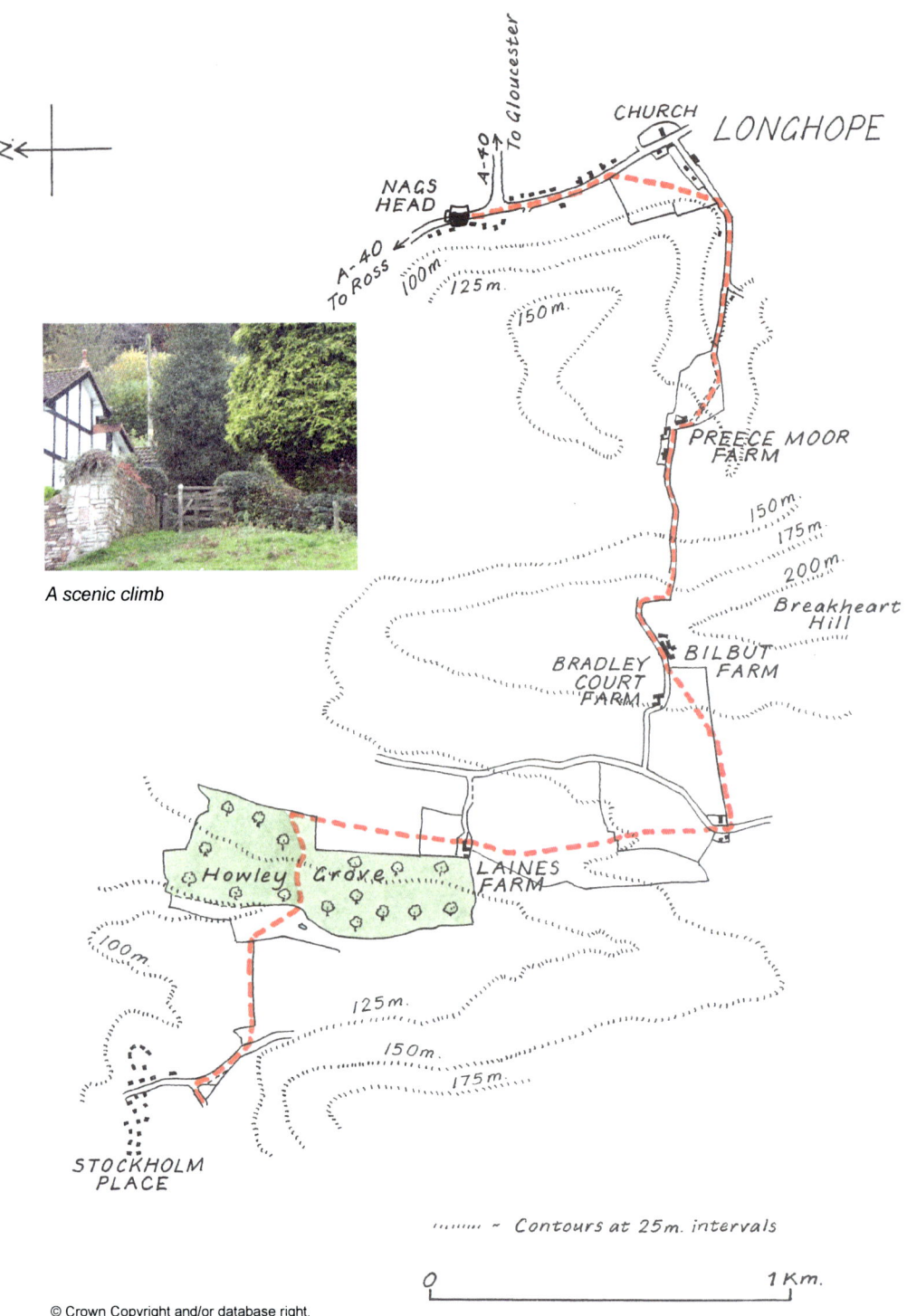

A scenic climb

making for the low roofed white house ahead. Enter the garden through a small wooden gate and cross over the driveway to a cattle grid with access road beyond.

Turn left and walk up to a gate into the farmyard of Laine's Farm and turn right. Then walk in front of large metal storage barns, to reach another gate on the far side. Cross the field towards woodland ahead and find an obscure stile on the outside edge of the wood. Cross this and walk for 100m into the wood but keeping the right hand boundary within a few metres. Arrive at a positive track and turn sharp left, (almost back on oneself) and follow this track as it leads back into the wood and arrives after about 200m at the inside corner of the wood with another cross track in front. Continue straight across this, down past holly bushes, to emerge at the bottom of the woodland by forestry work and horse jumps. **(14 km)**

Bear half right across the field (can be boggy at times) and make your way up to a metal gate which is in the hedge opposite and to the left of a venerable old oak tree with enormous girth. Pass through the gate into an arable field and follow the hedgerow on your left to a stile with awkward steps on the other side. Continue across a narrow field to another stile with a busy minor road beyond.

Turn right and walk for 200m up to a junction where turn left onto this quieter road **(15 km)** and walk for a further 200 metres up to another junction. Climb the bank on the opposite side and pass over a stile into a field with an attractive hamlet up on the hill above. Continue up to the right of a black and white house and pass through a gate into an enclosed path. Soon cross another path and continue up another enclosed path which passes two metal horse barriers. After the second barrier turn sharp right up steps to a lane.

Turn right on the lane and follow it around above houses with fine views across to the Malvern Hills. Ignore a trackway off to the left and continue on the lane as it drops down, quite steeply, to join a road. Turn left and after 100m fork right onto Combers Lane.

Initially walk downhill past an old railway bridge, **(16 km)** and then up towards a farm and houses. Just opposite a thatched cottage take a footpath with stile on the left and join a trackway which follows the hedge on the left and bends down to a large clearing with two gates ahead.

Take the left hand gate or stile alongside, climb up the bank alongside the hedge in the field beyond, and as the gradient eases bear half left across the field towards the tall Scots Pine trees in the distance. Find a metal gate, hidden but just before the trees, and emerge onto a lane. **(17 km)**

Turn left and walk past an old farmhouse, (watching and listening for cars approaching around the bend) and arrive at a footpath sign on the right opposite Rudge Cottages. Pass through two metal gates, drop down into a dip and then ascend up to a stile. Continue initially straight ahead up the bank but as one passes over the top, bear half left and walk down to the bottom corner by a hedge, to find a way marking sign and a small planked bridge over a stream.

Turn left and follow the hedge up to edge of woodland ahead. Enter the woodland and follow the faint track as it winds left and up to a vehicular trackway. Turn right and follow this to reach a junction of trackways. This area is known as Dancing Green, where turn right on a lane and continue, up over and down, to a road junction with a telephone box, just before on the right **(18 km)**.

Cross straight over at the junction and pass several attractive cottages and the access lane then becomes an enclosed path which can get quite overgrown but becomes easier as you enter woodland and after 200m arrive at a crossing track where turn right. Soon arrive at a stile and in the next small field bear half left downhill to a gap in the hedge and then in the next field make for the large pylon ahead.

Bear to the right of the pylon to reach a gate in new fencing and drop down to the left of a white painted cottage to arrive at a gate with access road beyond **(19 km)**.Turn left down the road which soon

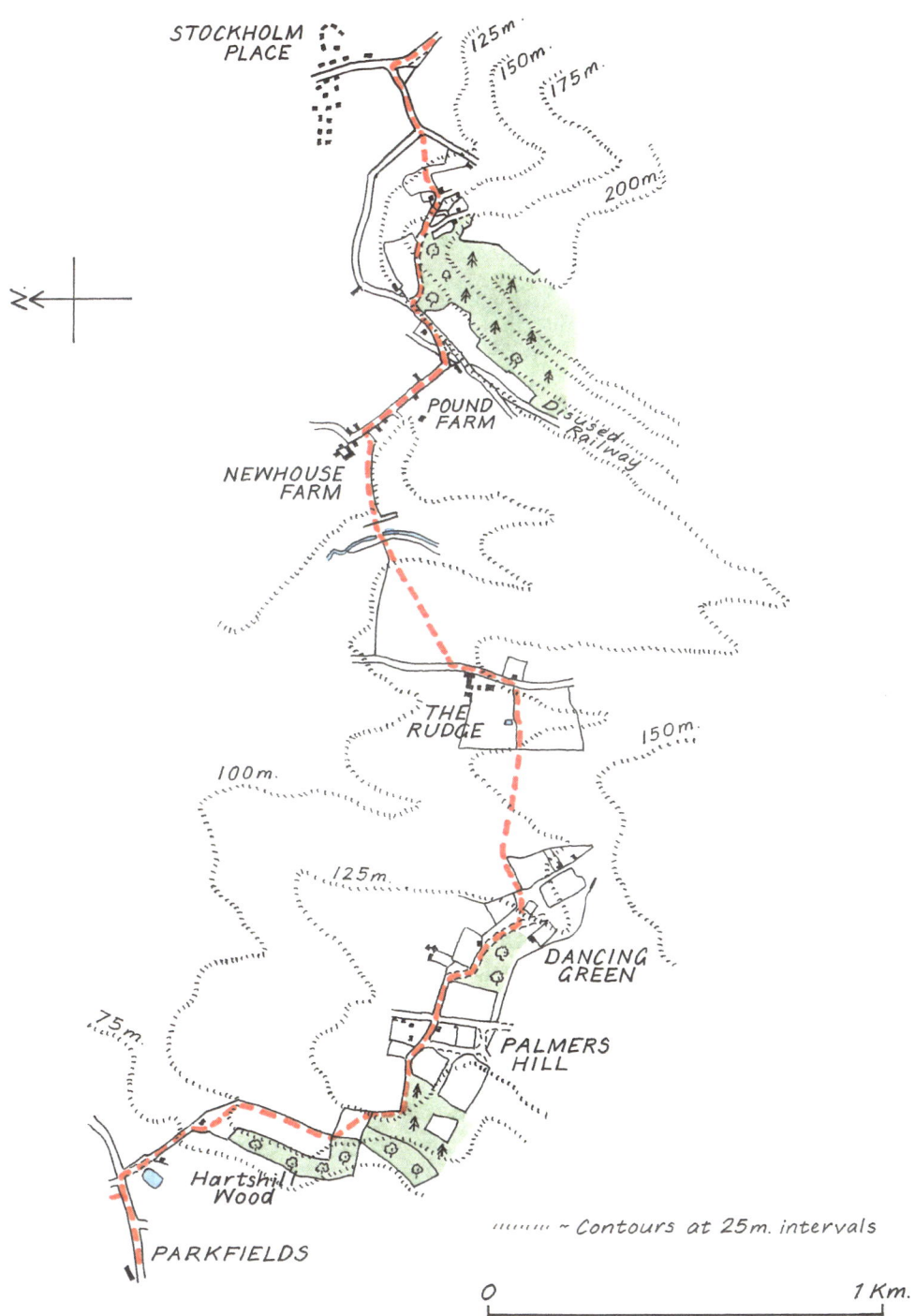

passes a substantial red brick smallholding and emerge on the minor road with Parkfields Country house along to the left and the route of the Original Ross Round emerging from the trackway opposite **(19.2 km)**

The Hope & Anchor

A family friendly Inn, in an outstanding location, where a warm and friendly welcome awaits you.

- **Separate Function Room available for hire**
- **Large riverside garden with ample seating**
- **Large free customer car park**

ALSO FEATURING
WYE LODGE B&B
2 Double Rooms
3 Twin Rooms
All rooms are en-suite.
Private car park and private garden overlooking the river.

Rope Walk • Ross-on-Wye
01989 563003

FOOD SERVED
every day, lunchtime and evenings

Good food and good service with a smile

Specials Board changed regularly

A wide range of freshly cooked meals and Bar snacks

The Ross Rounds

THE NEW MAY HILL LOOP
Overall distance 24.2km (15.13m)

STAGE 1
Connecting The Weston Inn to Hartleton 3km (1.88m)

STAGE 2
URR - Page 33 Hartleton to The Nags Head 10.0km (6.25m)

STAGE 3
URR - Page 37 Box Bush to Parkfields 9.0km (5.63m)

STAGE 4
Connecting Parkfields to The Weston Inn 2.0km (1.25m)

This provides a very interesting and challenging circular walk with May Hill the focal point and indeed visible for much of the route. The Nags Head Inn makes for a convenient lunchtime stop and both it and the Weston Cross Inn at Weston under Penyard are connected by the No33 Stagecoach bus service which runs on a regular basis between Gloucester and Ross on Wye.

In the event of bad weather or other circumstances this could enable walkers to settle for a half day walk and continue at another time, to return, either to The Weston Inn, or to continue from Parkfields on the ORR to Ross.

Route Description
STAGE 1
The Connecting Walk

Turn left outside the Weston Inn (Do not leave any car in the pub car park without permission) and walk up the lane. After approx 300m turn right into an access road and walk up to the end where, just before a drive to the end house, there is a footpath on the left.

This is actually an old "white road" and passes around several bends to emerge alongside the imposing Bollitree Lawns house and onto a lane. Turn left and walk up the lane past "The Old Rectory" and arrive at Bollitree Castle. The legend of this fortified farmhouse is described on Page 20 on The Original Ross Round (ORR) section .

Turn right at the junction and walk for 100m to find a footpath sign on the left. Pass through the double gates where the route is basically straight ahead with the aerial mast on the skyline a useful guide. This large field can often be in crop but there are usually lines free of crop heading in the general direction (NE). On reaching the bottom of the field there is a stile in the left boundary, under young trees, which cross and turn right up to a metal gate with stile.

Continue up the next field keeping close to the right hand boundary, Reach a stile in post and rail fencing and continue up to another metal gate with stile alongside. Pass a short section of enclosed path to reach another metal gate and road beyond.

Turn right and almost immediately left into a narrow lane. This leads downhill for about a km to reach the road from Hartleton where the original Ross Round route joins from Ross. Continue straight ahead down the lane which is now Stage 2 of The Ultimate Ross Round Page 33.

After completing **Stage 2 and 3 of The Ultimate Ross Round** arrive on a minor road with Parkfields Country House on your left.

STAGE 4
Connecting route back to Weston Inn at Weston under Penyard c2.0km

Cross the road onto a vehicular track way, continue uphill to pass a house on the left after 200m, and then look for a stile on the right in post and rail fencing. Cross this and follow the right hand boundary fence of this long and narrow field. Arrive after 500m at a stile in the corner which cross and continue on the same line until after another

300m cross over a ditch with a very awkward stile on the right into the adjoining field.

Bear left and make for the corner of the field with school buildings beyond. Cross over a track way and find a small timber gate on the opposite side into a field with the spire of Weston Church ahead. Follow the boundary hedge on the right to reach a stile which cross and continue on towards the church. Reach a wooden gate which pass through and then a metal one into the churchyard.

Exit from the churchyard by another metal gate on the right and drop down from the church to a lane. Turn right and continue down the lane to reach the busy A40 main road (note the bus stop on the right for Ross direction) and cross over carefully to The Weston Cross Inn.

The Bandstand at Ross Riverside

The Ross Rounds

The Alternative Return
From Ross to Weston Under Penyard

This enables walkers to achieve a circuit of 17.2km (10.75m) using this route back to Weston and then returning on the last section of The Original RR. It is particularly useful if walkers had previously stopped on the ORR at Weston and wished to complete the main route at another time.

ROSS to WESTON
Distance 5.2km (3.25m) allow 1.25 – 1.75 hours.

This is a pleasant little stage where, after initial urban walking, the route is soon up onto Chase Hill and has a variety of interesting features before descending back down through Penyard Park to Weston.

Cross the road opposite The Riverside Inn and take the path alongside the public conveniences that winds uphill alongside the gardens to woodland. At the top, turn left through the bollards, then turn right, and walk along the pavement before crossing over the road to join an obvious footpath opposite, which ascends the hillside underneath the red sandstone cliffs.

Reach a junction of paths and continue ahead through cycle barriers. The track soon becomes tarmac and continue ahead past Ashfield Park School to arrive at a busy road junction. Cross over into Palmerston Road and take the first road on the right which is Ashfield Crescent. This winds around to reach the main (Walford) road **(1km)**.

Turn right, walk along the pavement for 200m, then cross over to Eastfield Road, and then immediately bear right into Fernbank Road. Continue up this road, which after 300m, becomes unsurfaced and then ascends quite steeply to a junction of tracks at the top. Proceed left of centre to a metalled gate with waymarking signs and continue

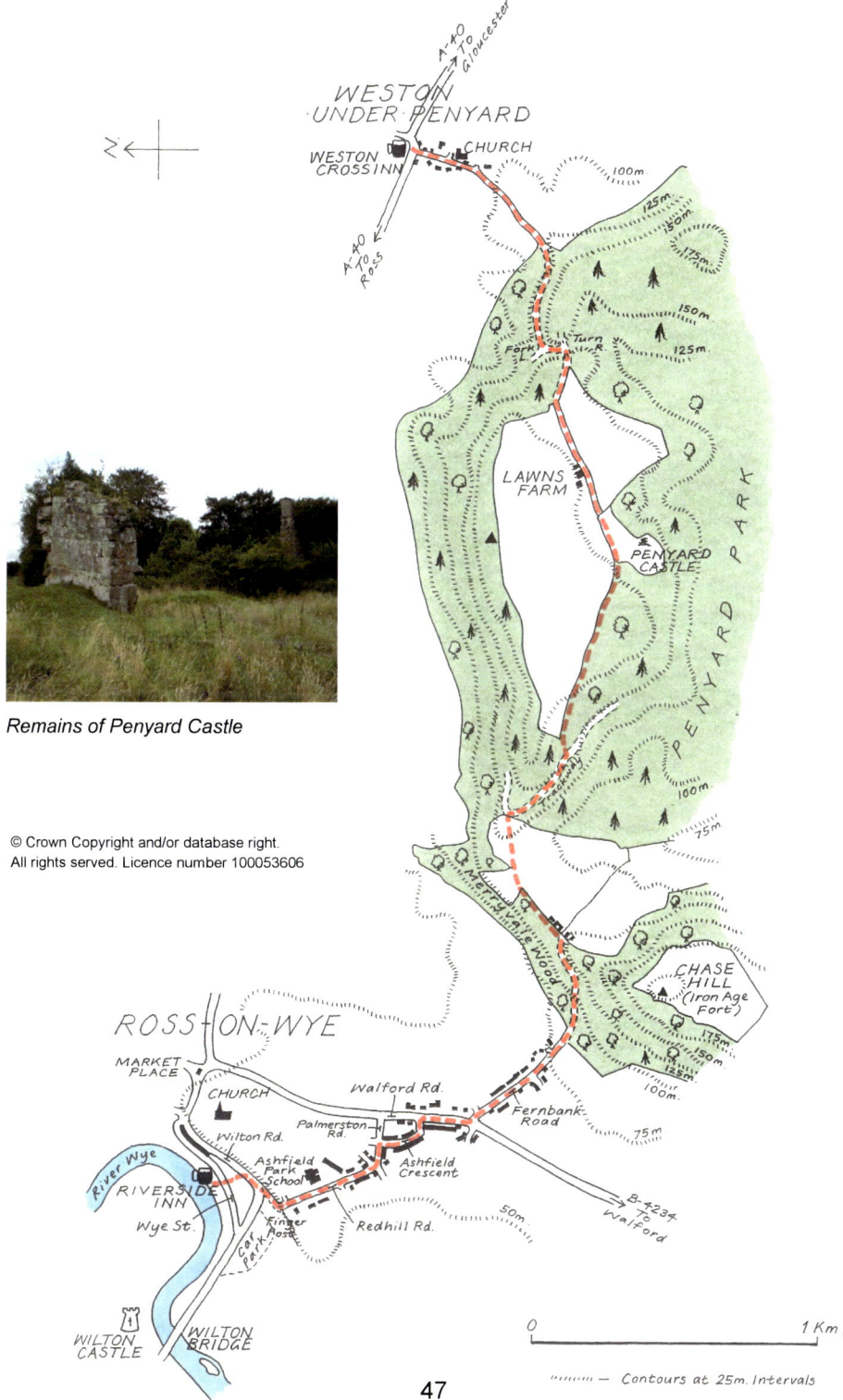

Remains of Penyard Castle

through into the wood. After 50m bear right at a fork and proceed to a stile on the edge of the wood with a rather nice stone commemorative bench alongside **(2km)**.Arrive on the large open grassed area and follow the fence on the right as it bends right up to woodland. Cross a stile and arrive on a broad trackway where turn right and proceed uphill for 300m until, as the gradient levels out, there is a footpath on the left. This leads uphill (again!) through gorse bushes and then continues on as it passes through holly bushes **(3km)** where from this high point (nearly 200m) there is an unexpected view of May Hill in the distance.

Descend to a stile with a large field where beyond, on the far side of the field, are the remaining ruins of Penyard Castle which once had a commanding situation over the valleys below. Turn left and walk towards Lawn Farm passing through two gates on the way and arriving on a stone track way by the farmhouse. Continue on the track way through another gate to arrive after a further 200m at a junction of tracks **(4km)** where turn left and follow the main track downhill for 100m and then fork right at the junction.This track way arrives, after just under a kilometre, alongside Weston Church **(5km)**. Those walkers wishing to use all the facilities at The Weston Inn should continue on down the lane to the busy A40 where the pub is opposite (5.2km- 3.25m) There is also a bus stop on either side of the main road for the hourly Gloucester- Ross service. Those walkers who have either arrived too early for the pub to be open or who wish to return to Ross on foot, without any delay, can turn up to the church and join the main ORR without dropping down to the A40 and pub.

The Loughpool Loop

Distance 19.2 km (12.0m)
allow 4.5- 5.5 hours without stops

This is an attractive and easy going circuit which explores the countryside on the other side of the river Wye from Ross and makes use of the Herefordshire Trail for most of the return from The Loughpool Inn.

Leave Ross by The Riverside Inn on the same route as The Original Ross Round ORR (see page 12) and follow it until arriving on a lane by the suspension bridge over the river (see page 14, para 4) **(5.5km)**

Cross over the bridge which is almost identical to another bridge further up stream by Sellack. Turn sharp left on the far side and follow the path alongside the river with Foy Church, clearly ahead. Arrive at a metal gate, **(6km)** and cross over the field to ascend steps up to this attractive and isolated church. There are two benches outside to enjoy a rest and to admire the view over the river and for those wishing to see the inside of the church (Norman origins) the front door is on the opposite, north, side. The title of Foy has recently been adopted by the, now ennobled, Labour government minister Peter Mandelson.

Leave the churchyard by the north side, walk through the car park and out onto the lane where turn right. Follow the lane out of the village until at the far side of a farm building there is a footpath on the left. Follow the left hand boundary of the field, initially around the farm buildings but then up towards the ridge ahead **(7km)**

Arrive at the top corner and find a gate the other side of a brick "tump". Turn left and follow the hedge up to another gate and the path becomes a trackway with great views all around and the Welsh hills in the distance. The trackway then moves through a gap into the left hand field but continues ahead on the same line towards farm buildings.**(8km)**

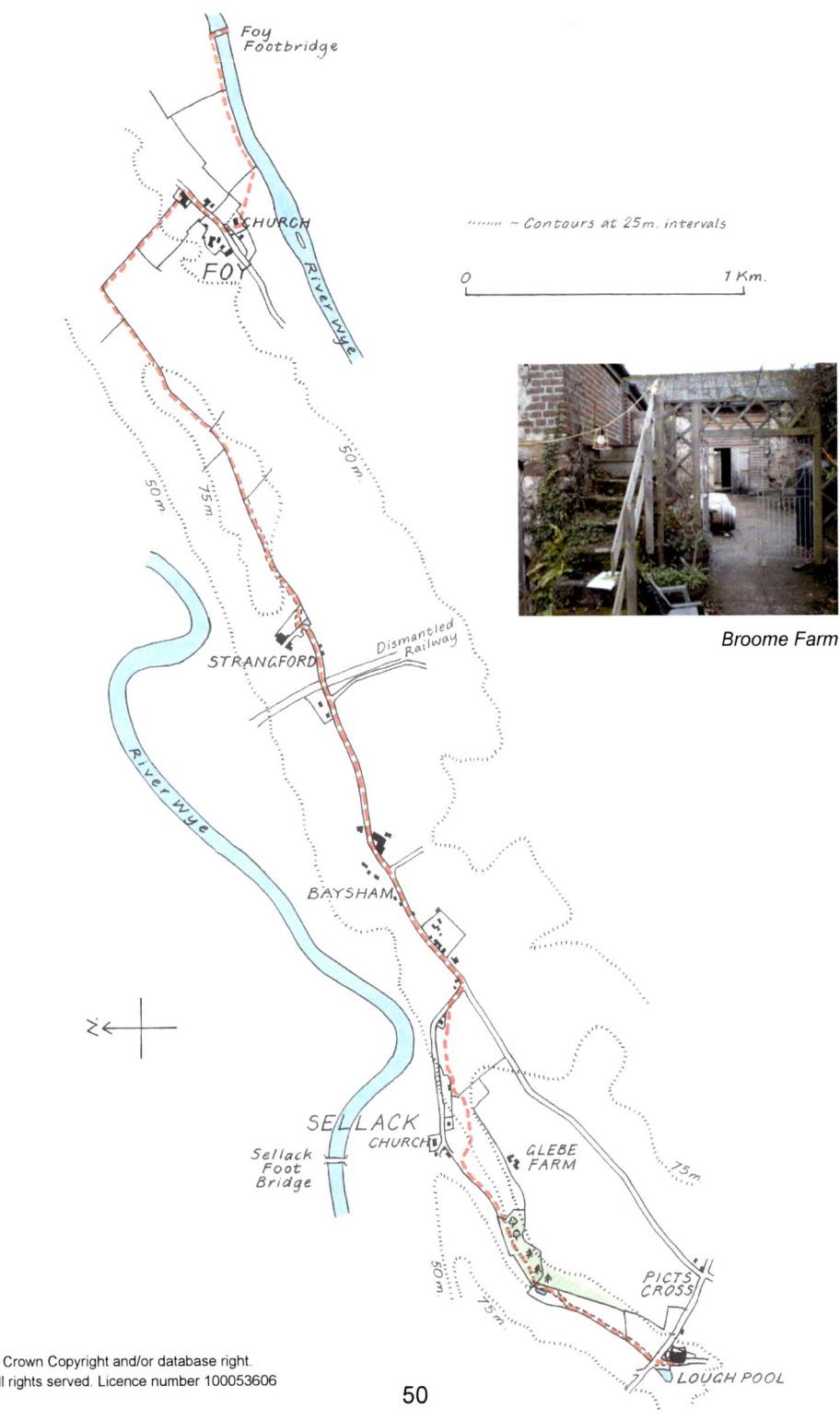

Broome Farm

Walk through the farmyard and join an access lane on the far side. Turn left and follow the lane down past cottages including a rather nice conversion with exposed timbers and 24 solar heating panels on the roof! **(9km)** Continue on the lane for another 500m and reach a road to continue ahead past a very old barn with "arrow" apertures, to reach a T junction.**(10km)**

Turn right SP Sellack Church and after 100m turn off to the left at a waymark post and follow a path in the field alongside the right hand boundary. This passes two rather nicely converted houses with good elevated views over the river below. Reach a stile in the top corner, Cross over and reach a further stile some 20m further down on the right hand side. Cross this and follow the enclosed path down through the trees to reach another stile in about 200m.

Cross the stile into a long narrow field and initially make towards the opposite side but then bear left and walk up the field to a large wooded gate with a smaller pedestrian gate and stile alongside **(11km)**. After 10m turn right onto a narrower track and after another 10m bear right again onto a further track. Turn left and follow the stream on your left, through pasture and on to a large wooden field gate.

Continue on up the next large field but before the end bear up right to reach a wooden pedestrian gate on the bank. Pass through an enclosed area to cross a bridge and then pass through another gate onto a minor road. Turn left and arrive at the old and atmospheric Loughpool Inn **(11.5km)**.

After, hopefully, enjoying all the facilities of the pub, walk back through the car park to the road, turn right, and walk up the hill for 200m to find a footpath sign on the right hand side. You have now joined The Herefordshire Trail which you will **mostly** follow all the way back to Ross. Cross straight over the field from the stile making for another stile on the opposite side. Walk across the lawn of the house to cross a driveway where continue up ahead through a gap. Cross an access trackway and continue up through another gap and through an enclosed area to reach a lane.

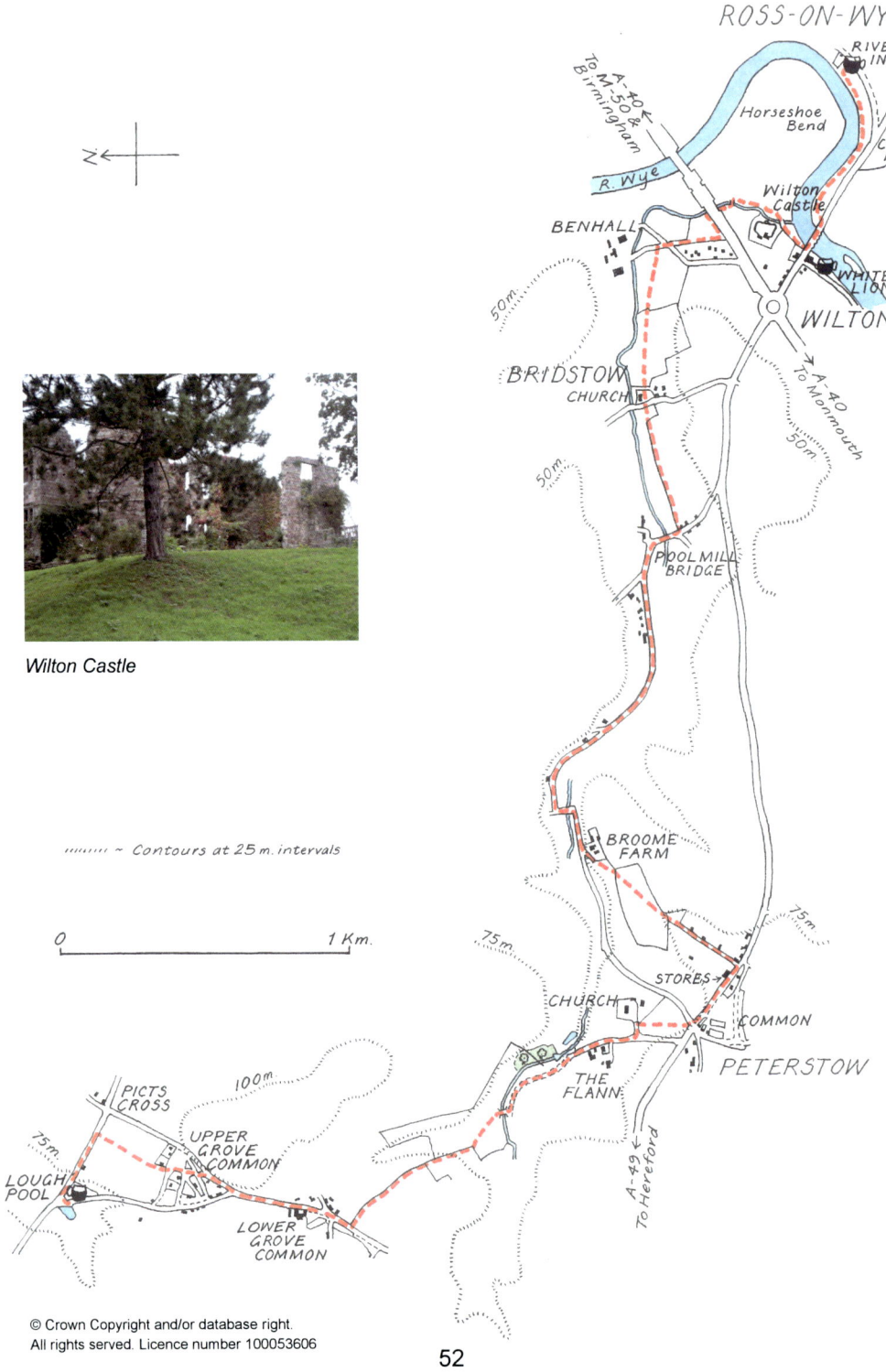

Turn right and follow the lane down to a junction SP Gluestone and Pencraig. Continue straight ahead to another junction SP Peterstone **(12km)** and continue ahead for 100m and find a new gate on the left and pass into a large field. Follow the left hand boundary through two fields, with gates, and then in the third field make your way across and down to a stile opposite.(13km) Pass through a narrow piece of woodland to cross a bridge and arrive over another stile into a large field. Turn left and follow the boundary around towards large farm buildings ahead **(14km)**.

Turn off the path just before the buildings and pass through a metal gate and proceed uphill to an access trackway to the farm. Join a lane and immediately turn left down towards Whitehouse Farm. Just before the entrance turn right and ascend steps to a stile and cross the field opposite to reach a stile on the far side.

Arrive on the edge of the very busy A49, turn left and cross a lane (Herefordshire Way leaves here) and continue on the pavement alongside the A49. Pass the post office and stores and almost immediately turn left down an access lane **(15km)**.

At the end of the houses continue ahead on a trackway into a very large cider orchard and continue on it as it bears left downhill to reach an access lane to Broome Farm. (see separate advert for this thriving business) Pass the entrance to the farm and arrive on a busy lane where turn right. Continue along the lane, to pass cottages **(16km)** and reach a junction with a larger road where fork right SP Ross on Wye.

Continue over another junction and a bridge where soon after and just before a prominent white house, take a footpath on the left. Pass though a metal kissing gate and continue towards a church ahead **(17km)**. Continue through two more gates to arrive at a lane in front of the church and pass through the churchyard to another gate on the far side.

Continue straight ahead across this long field through two more gates to find a further gate on the far side which is initially hidden from view but make for buildings to arrive out onto an access lane. Turn right but after 30m turn left at a finger post and cross the track to a gate on the side of the house **(18km)**. Follow the path as it leads around the back of the house, then pass through a metal kissing gate and walk down through pasture to the far right of four tunnels under the A40 trunk road. Emerge on the other side and continue ahead with a brook on the left and the ruins of Wilton Castle ahead.

Cross over the brook on a substantial wooden bridge and immediately turn right to walk alongside the castle. Reach a smaller concrete bridge which cross, pass through a metal kissing gate and then turn left and walk ahead towards the prominent road bridge where turn right and ascend steps up onto the bridge.

Turn left and follow the pavement across this long bridge where soon there is a choice of routes **(19km)**. If returning to The Riverside Inn and Ross town centre then turn left off the pavement, down steps, and onto The John Kyrle Walk which leads across the meadows alongside the river. In very wet weather, when the meadows can be flooded, it can be better to continue along the pavement and then onto the access road to the Riverside area. Before reaching the access road, the entrance to the Wilton Road (free) car park will be seen on the right where no doubt many walkers may have left their vehicles **(19.2km-12m)**.

The Lough Pool Inn

Sellack, Ross on Wye, Hereford, HR9 6LX
Tel: 01989 730888
Email: info@theloughpoolinn.co.uk
www.theloughpoolinn.co.uk

Come and enjoy a traditional country pub unspoilt by time with oak beams, flagstone floors and real open fires

- **Extensive choice of locally sourced wholesome food with at least five vegetarian options on every day**
- **Two cask ales, a range of local ciders and choice of popular wines to compliment your meal**
- **Sunday Roast as a special every week**
- **Chef's Lunchtime Specials Tuesday to Friday**

Food served:
Tuesday – Saturday 12.00-2.00pm and 6.30-9.30pm
Sundays – 12.00-2.30pm
BOOKINGS ADVISABLE WEEKENDS